Sounds All Around:
A Child's Bible
Alphabet Reader

By E. X. Caelo

Self published by: E. X. Caelo

ISBN: 979-8-89379-590-5

Edition/Printing: First Edition, July 2025

For permissions requests, write to the publisher at: contact@micaias.org

Printed in the United States of America

Now unto him that is able to keep you from falling, and to present you faultless before the presence of his glory with exceeding joy...

—Jude 24

Dear Parents,

It is my sincere desire that this small book may be a delight to your little one(s) both visually and audibly as well as an aid in helping your child(ren) to identify common sounds that we hear in our alphabet. As I compiled this book, I realized it might be helpful to have separate pages for sound combinations such as "TH", "SH", and "CH". While I have not covered every sound combination (for example I omitted "ng" and "ph") my hope is that you may point out these special sound combinations in your reading with your child. May the Lord bless His word to the hearts of our little ones as we raise them up in the way that they should go.

Blessings,

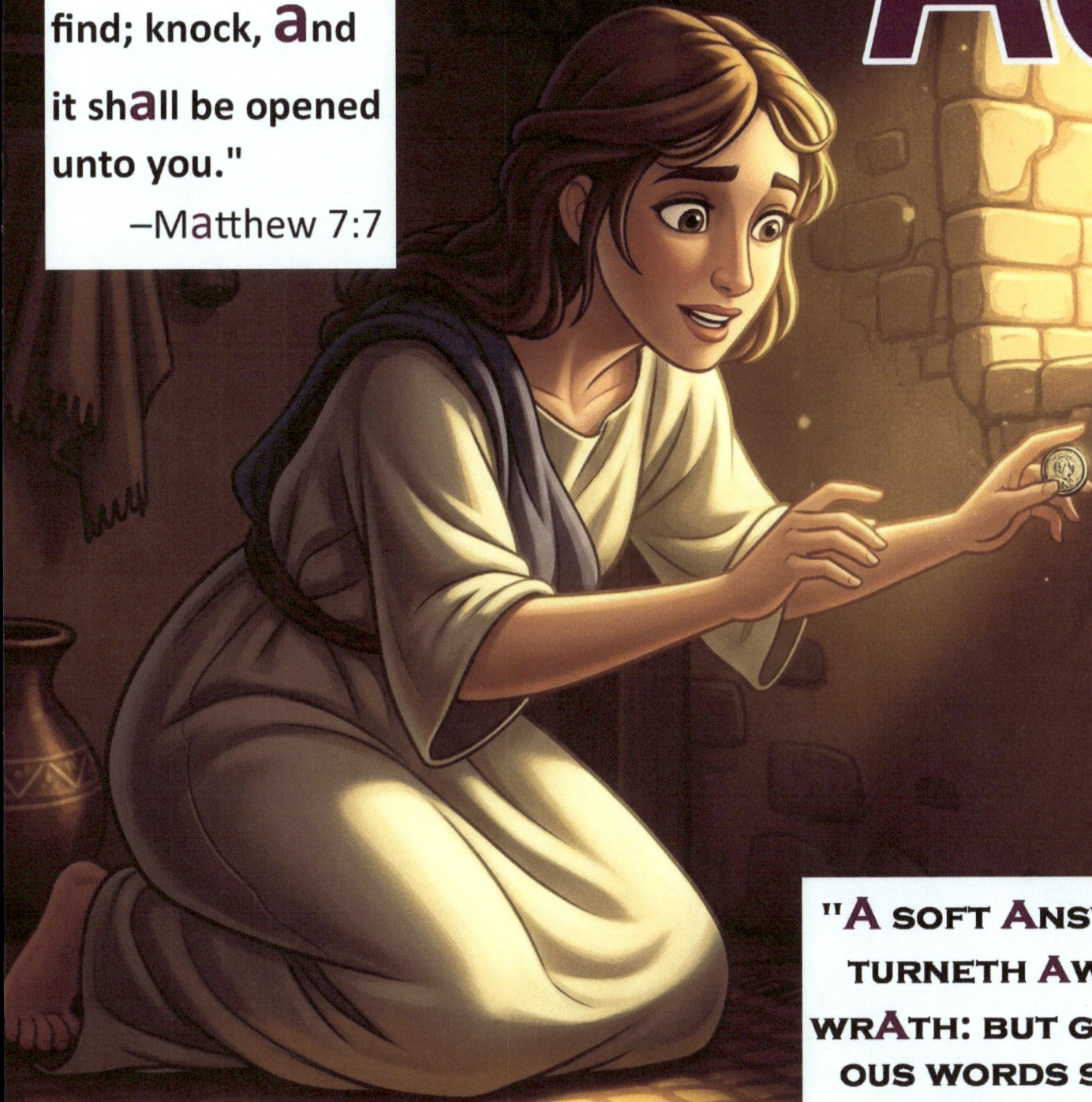

"**A**sk, and it sh**a**ll be given you; seek, **a**nd ye sh**a**ll find; knock, **a**nd it sh**a**ll be opened unto you."
—Matthew 7:7

Aa

"**A** SOFT **A**NSWER TURNETH **A**WAY WR**A**TH: BUT GRIEVOUS WORDS STIR UP **A**NGER."
—PROVERBS 15:1

Bb

"**B**eloved, let us love one another: for love is of God."
—1 John 4:7

"**B**lessed are the merciful: for they shall o**b**tain mercy." —Matthew 5:7

Cc

Cast thy burden upon the LORD, and he shall sustain thee: he shall never suffer the righteous to be moved.

–Psalms 55:22

"Come unto me, all ye that labour and are heavy laden, and I will give you rest."

–Matthew 11:28

CH

"Children, obey your parents in the Lord: for this is right." —Ephesians 6:1

Chasten thy son while there is hope, and let not thy soul spare for his crying. —Proverbs 19:18

D d

"**D**o all things without murmurings an**d** **d**isputings."
–Philippians 2:14

"**D**elight thyself also in the LORD; and he shall give thee the **d**esires of thine heart."
–Psalm 37:4

Ee

"Even a child is known by his do-ings, whether his work *be* pure, and whether *it be* right."

–Proverbs 20:11

"Every good gift and every perfect gift is from above."

–James 1:17

"Forgive, and ye shall be forgiven."   —Luke 6: 37

"A friend loveth at all times, and a brother is born for adversity."
—Proverbs 17:17

Ff

"**G**od is our refuge and strength, a very present help in trouble."
—Psalm 46:1

Gg

"**G**ive, and it shall be **g**iven unto you."
—Luke 6:38

Hh

"He that dwelleth in the secret place of the most High shall abide under the shadow of the Almighty."

–Psalm 91:1

"Hold fast that which is good."   –1 Thessalonians 5:21

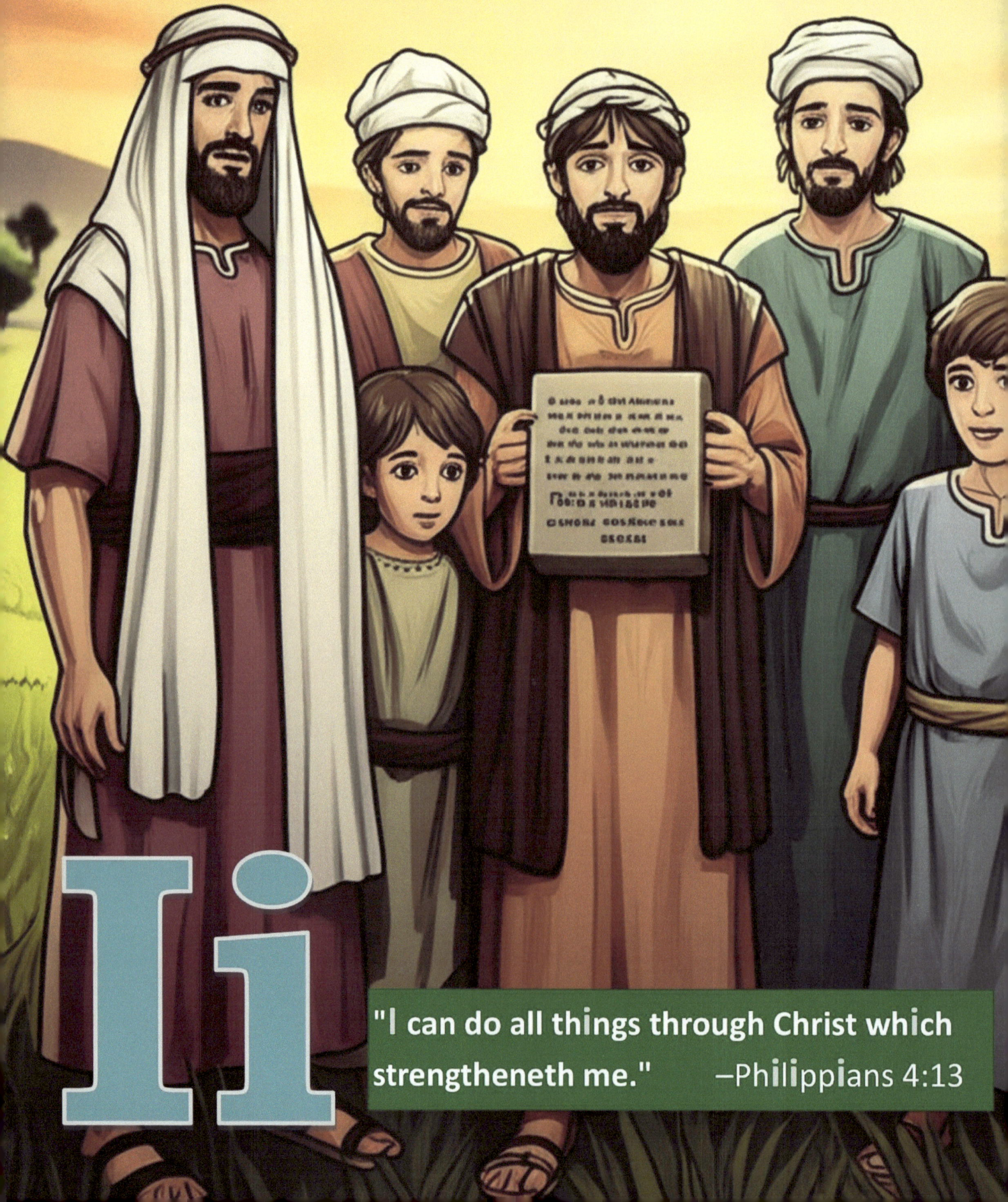

"If ye love me, keep my commandments." —John 14:15

Ii

"I can do all things through Christ which strengtheneth me." —Philippians 4:13

"**J**udge not, that ye be not **j**udged."
–Matthew 7:1

Jj

It is **j**oy to the **j**ust to do **j**udgment: but destruction shall be to the workers of iniquity.
—Proverbs 21:15

"**K**eep thy heart with all diligence;
for out of it are the issues of life."
—Proverbs 4:23

Kk

Keep the sabbath day to sanctify it,
as the LORD thy God hath command-
ed thee.   —Deuteronomy 5:12

"**L**et your **l**ight so shine before men that they may see your good works and g**l**orify your father which is in heaven." —Matthew 5:16

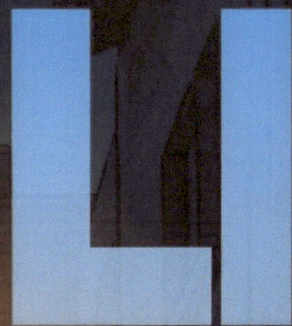

Ll

"**L**ove the **L**ORD thy God with a**ll** thine heart." —Deuteronomy 6:5

Mm

"**M**y help co**m**eth fro**m** the LORD which **m**ade heaven and earth."

—Psal**m** 121:2

"**M**ercy and truth are **m**et together."   —Psal**m** 85:10

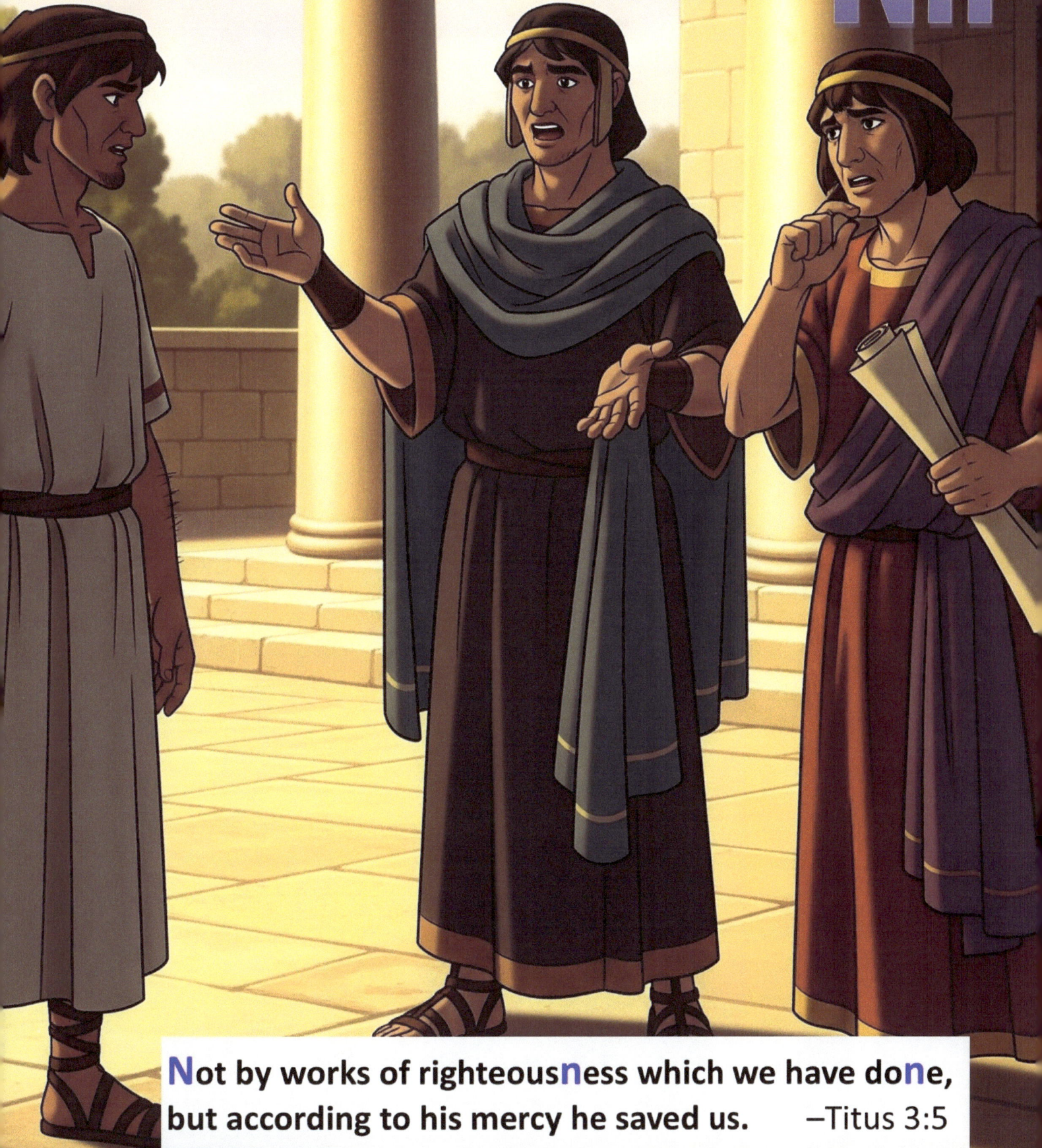

"No man can serve two masters."   —Matthew 6:24

Nn

Not by works of righteousness which we have done, but according to his mercy he saved us.   —Titus 3:5

"**O**pen th**o**u mine eyes, that I may beh**o**ld w**o**ndr**o**us things **o**ut of thy law."

—Psalm 119:18

"**O** taste and see that the LORD is g**oo**d."

—Psalm 34:8

"**P**ray without ceasing."
    –1 Thessalonians 5:17

Pp

"**P**eace I leave with you, my **p**eace I give unto you."
    –John 14:27

"Let everyone be **q**uick to hear, slow to speak, slow to wrath."   —James 1:19

"**Q**uench not the Spirit."
   —1 Thessalonians 5:19

Qq

"**R**emember the sabbath day, to keep it holy."
—Exodus 20:8

"**R**ejoice in the Lo**r**d alway: and again I say, **R**ejoice." —Philippians 4:4

Rr

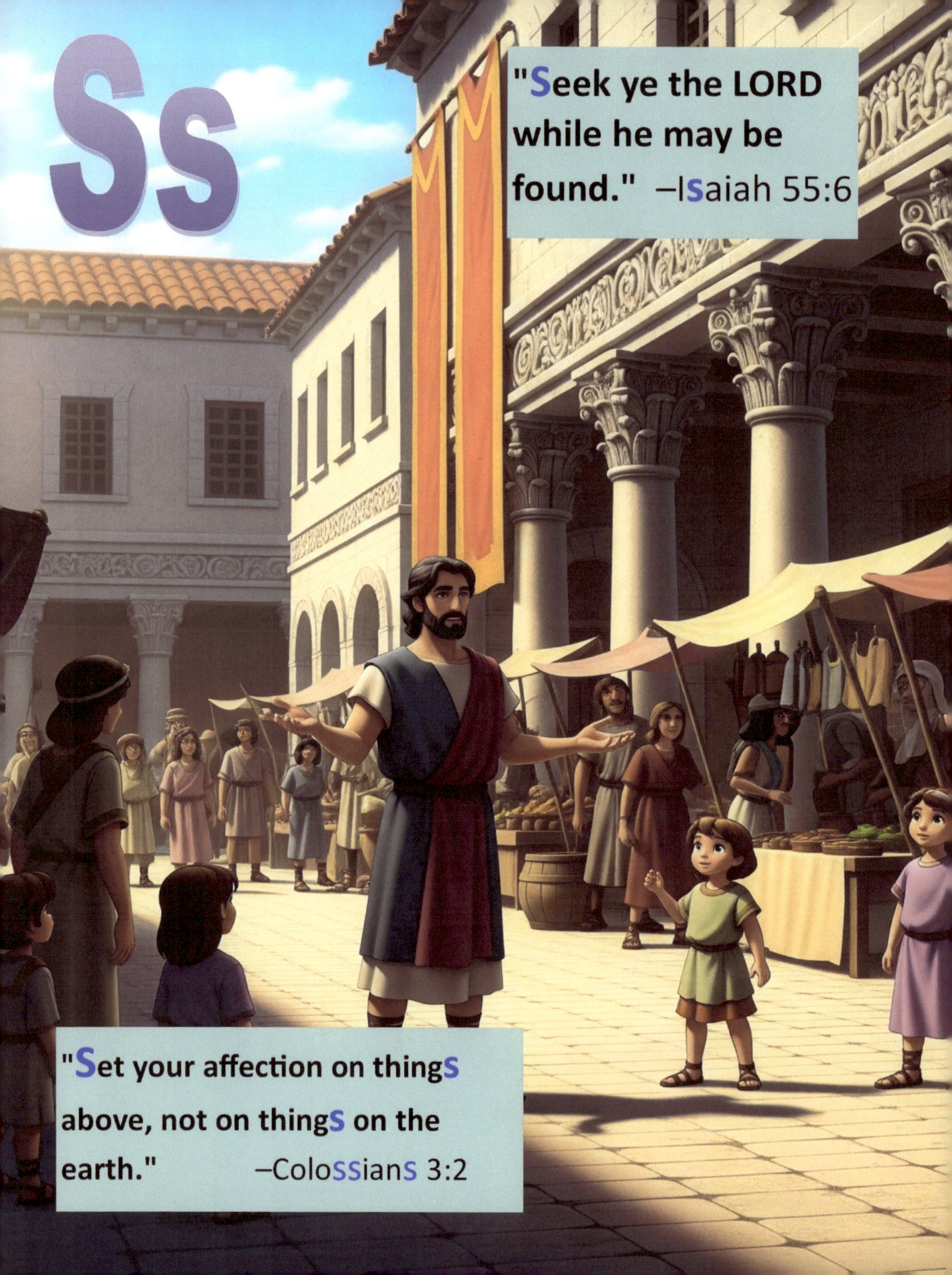

Ss

"**S**eek ye the LORD while he may be found." —I**s**aiah 55:6

"**S**et your affection on thing**s** above, not on thing**s** on the earth." —Colo**ss**ian**s** 3:2

My **sh**eep hear my voice, and I know them, and they follow me: –John 10:27

SH

The Lord is my **sh**epherd; I **sh**all not want. –Psalm 23:1

"**Trust in the LORD with all thine heart and lean not on your own understanding.**"
—Proverbs 3:5

Tt

To him that overcometh will I grant to sit with me in my throne, even as I also overcame, and am set down with my Father in his throne.
—Revelation 3:21

Therefore shall a man leave his father and his mother, and shall cleave unto his wife: and they shall be one flesh. —Genesis 2:24

TH

"Thy word is a lamp unto my feet, and a light unto my path." —Psalm 119:105

Uu

"**U**nto thee, O LORD, do I lift **u**p my soul."
—Psalm 25:1

Unto Adam also and to his wife did the LORD God make coats of skins, and clothed them.
—Genesis 3:21

Vex the Midianites, and smite them:
—Numbers 25:17

Vow, and pay unto the LORD your God: let all that be round about him bring presents unto him that ought to be feared. —Psalm 76:11

Ww

We remember the fish, which We did eat in Egypt freely; the cucumbers, and the melons, and the leeks, and the onions, and the garlick:
—Numbers 11:5

"Wait on the LORD: be of good courage."
—Psalm 27:14

Whosoever hateth his brother is a murderer: and ye know that no murderer hath eternal life abiding in him. –1 John 3:15

WH

Who is a wise man and endued with knowledge among you? let him shew out of a good conversation his works with meekness of wisdom. –James 3:13

Xx

E**X**CEPT THE LORD BUILD THE HOUSE THEY LABOR IN VAIN THAT BUILD IT. —PSALM 127:1

E**X**cept the Lord keep the city, the watchmen labor but in vain.   —Psalm 127:2

Ye are the salt of the earth: but if the salt have lost his savor, wherewith shall it be salted? it is thenceforth good for nothing, but to be cast out, and to be trodden under foot of men.

—Matthew 5 :13

Yy

Ye are the light of the world. A city that is set on an hill cannot be hid.

—Matthew 5:14

Zebulun shall dwell at the haven of the sea; and he shall be for an haven of ships; and his border shall be unto **Z**idon.

—Genesis 49:13

ZEBULUN

Zz

Zion heard, and was glad; and the daughters of Judah rejoiced because of thy judgments, O **Lord**.

—Psalm 97:8

www.ingramcontent.com/pod-product-compliance
Lightning Source LLC
LaVergne TN
LVHW072109070426
835509LV00002B/87